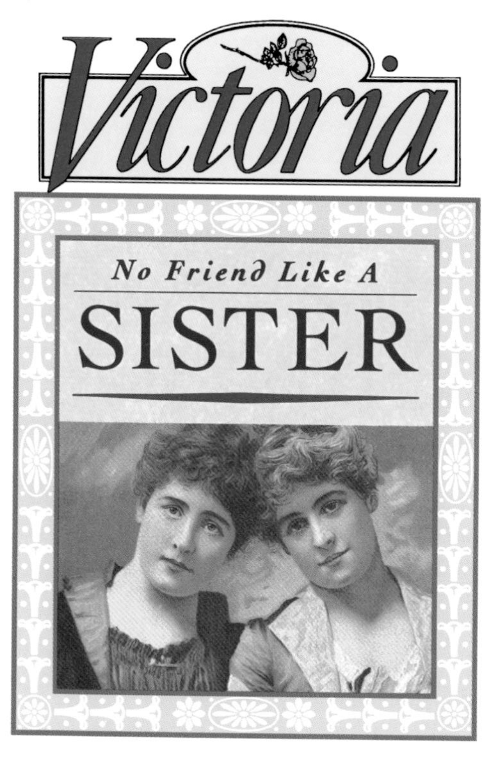

HEARST BOOKS
NEW YORK

All permissions and copyright credits appear on pages 138-143. Recognizing the importance of preserving what has been written, it is the policy of William Morrow and Company, Inc., and its imprints and affiliates to have the books it publishes printed on acid-free paper, and we exert our best efforts to that end.

Victoria, no friend like a sister

p. cm.

A collection of recollections from many generations of writers enhanced by quotations and illustrations from Victoria magazine. Published in a journal format so that readers can chronicle their own recollections.

ISBN: 0-688-10624-2

1. Sisters—Literary collections. 2. Friendship—Literary collections.

I. Victoria (New York, N.Y.) II. Title: No friend like a sister.

PN6071.S425V53 1993 92–27649 CIP

Printed in Singapore

First U.S. Edition

1 2 3 4 5 6 7 8 9 10

For Victoria -

Nancy Lindemeyer, Editor

Bryan E. McCay, Art Director

John Mack Carter, Director, Magazine Development

Edited by Linda Sunshine

Designed by Nina Ovryn

Produced by Smallwood & Stewart, Inc., New York City

NOTICE: Every effort has been made to locate the copyright owners of the material used in this book. Please let us know if an error has been made, and we will make any necessary changes in subsequent printings.

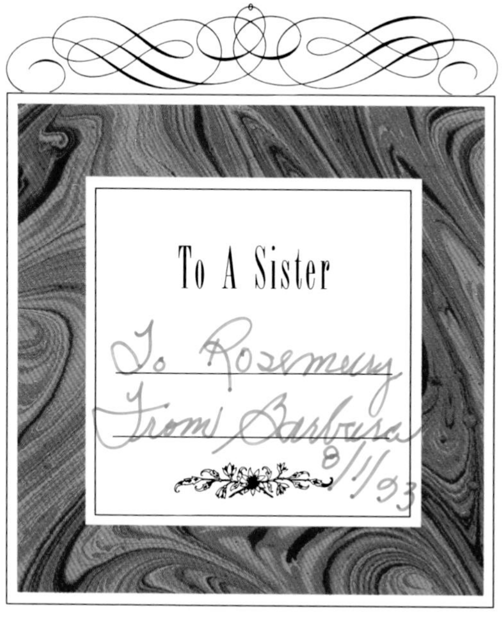
To A Sister
To Rosemary
From Barbara
8/1/93

INTRODUCTION

Our magazine, *Victoria,* has always maintained a special reverence for the joys of family and the magical, sometimes mystical, bonds that exist between family members. In a world fraught with ambiguity and uncertainty, we find the greatest solace and comfort from the people closest to us, and we believe that the bonds between sisters are among the most powerful. A sister is more than a friend or companion; she

INTRODUCTION

is a mirror wherein we see the reflection of ourselves, both as adults and as the children we once were.

George Eliot once wrote: "It is hard to believe that anything is worthwhile, unless there is some eye to kindle in common with our own, some brief word uttered now and then to imply that what is infinitely precious to us is precious alike to another person." For many of us, a sister is the person with whom we first share what is infinitely precious.

It is our hope that through the pages of this book, women will explore their deepest feelings about being a sister and the relationship that has somehow shaped and guided their lives. At the same time, by adding your own personal observations and feelings, you will be creating a family heirloom to share with your sister and to pass down to future generations.

***The Editors,* Victoria**

For there is no friend like a sister
In calm and stormy weather;
To cheer one on the tedious way,
To fetch one if one goes astray,
To lift one if one totters down,
To strengthen whilst one stands.

Christina Rosetti
Goblin Market

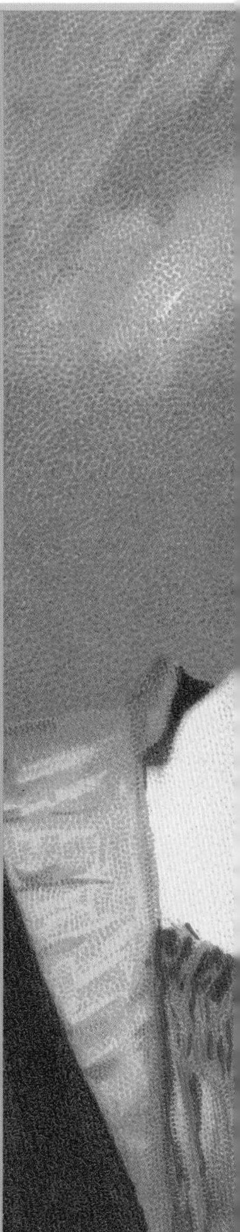

When I was young,
we *always* had mornings like this.

A.A. Milne
Toad of Town Hall

Life in common among people who love each other is the ideal of happiness.

George Sand
Histoire de Ma Vie

For what am I here for
If not to link fingers
With daughters whose wistfulness
Worlds never answer?
For what is a song for
If not to stretch hands out
To signal the falling,
"You're never alone"?

Peter Viereck
To Be Sung

How dear to this heart are the scenes of my childhood,
When fond recollection presents them to view!

Samuel Woodworth
The Old Oaken Bucket

Earliest Recollections of My Sister

We shall walk in velvet shoes:
Wherever we go
Silence will fall like dews
On white silence below.

Elinor Wylie
Velvet Shoes

I can't think I had much of a sense of humor as long as I remained the only child. When my brother Edward came along after I was three, we both became comics, making each other laugh. We set each other off, as we did for life, from the minute he learned to talk. A sense of the absurd was communicated between us probably before that.

Eudora Welty
One Writer's Beginnings

I have a little shadow that goes in and out with me,
And what can be the use of him is more than I can see.
He is very, very like me from the heels up to the head;
And I see him jump before me, when I jump into my bed.

Robert Louis Stevenson
My Shadow

Shared Moments with My Sister

*Suzanne took the arrival
of a sister with alternating disdain and
interest. Big for her age at four,
she did tend to hug the baby so hard that Claire,
at first delighted, would scream and
cry until a parent came to pry her from
the squeeze; and yet she
never shrank from Suzanne's touch.*

Joan Silber
Household Words

All older children feel that they are
"not good enough" when a younger sibling is born.
Not, somehow, "up to snuff." They
come to feel that somehow they were born a
"Ford Pinto," and are in effect being
"recalled by the manufacturer." Maybe you
tried to look closely at the face of your sister at
birth, and it looked like a stewed grape, and you
thought, "This is an improvement?"

Stephanie Brush
Life: A Warning

They could see she was a real princess and no question about it, now that she had felt one pea all the way through twenty mattresses and twenty more feather beds. Nobody but a princess could be so delicate.

Hans Christian Andersen
The Princess and the Pea

We were standing where
there was a fine view of the harbor
and its long stretches of shore all
covered by the great army of
the pointed firs, darkly cloaked and
standing as if they waited to embark.
As we looked far seaward among the
outer islands, the trees seemed to
march seaward still, going steadily
over the heights and down to the
water's edge.

Sarah Orne Jewett
The Country of the Pointed Firs

One bright summer night, when we were very small and the humid air hung like moss over the lowcountry, my sister and brother and I could not sleep. Our mother took us out of the house . . . and walked all of us down to the river and out onto the dock . . . . "There's something I want you to see. Something that will help you sleep. Look over there, children," she said, pointing out toward the horizon to the east.

It was growing dark on this long southern evening and suddenly, at the exact point her finger had indicated, the moon lifted a forehead of stunning gold above the horizon, lifted straight out of filigreed, light-intoxicated clouds that lay on the skyline in attendant veils . . . .

We children sat transfixed before that moon our mother had called forth from the waters. When the moon had reached its deepest silver, my sister, Savannah, though only three, cried aloud to our mother, to Luke and me, to the river and the moon, "Oh, Mama, do it again!" And I had my earliest memory.

Pat Conroy
The Prince of Tides

Family Memories

Now as I was young and easy under the apple bough

About the lilting house and happy as the grass was green.

***Dylan Thomas*, Fern Hill**

HOW TO TORTURE YOUR SISTER

She ate her jelly doughnut at lunch. You saved yours. It is now two hours later:

Sit down next to your sister on the couch. Put the jelly doughnut on a napkin in your lap. Leave it, untouched, until she asks you if you still want it. Then begin eating. "Mmmmmmmmmmmmm. This is soooooooooo good." Take a large bite and chew with mouth open so she gets a good view. Swallow and run tongue over lips. "Mmmmmmmmmmmmm." Stick tongue in jelly center and wave it around in the air before pulling it back in mouth. "Don't you wish you had some?" Take tiny bites. Lick fingers in between. "Boy—there's nothing like having a jelly doughnut in the middle of the afternoon!" Pop last bite in mouth and pat stomach.

Wander into the room when she calls a friend on the telephone. Pick up a book and sit down on the couch. Pretend to

read. Then mimic her as she begins her telephone conversation.

Hi, how are you? *Hi, how are you*. Wha'd you do today? *Wha'd you do today?* What? Wait a minute, my sister's driving me crazy. Would you cut it out. *Would you cut it out*. You dirty creep. *You dirty creep*. Stop repeating me! *Stop repeating me!* I'll kill you if you don't stop! *I'll kill you if you don't stop!* I said STOP! *I said STOP!* STOP IT!!!! *STOP IT!!!!*

Put down book and run.

She is eating peanuts. Whisper in her ear, "You can turn into an elephant if you eat too many peanuts. I read it in the World Book."

Follow her everywhere.

Imitate her best friend talking. Say that her best friend is fat.

Talk to your mother while your sister is listening:

"Do you remember Christmas when I was three years old and you gave me that stuffed animal? That was so much fun." Turn to your sister: "You weren't alive."

You are in bed with the flu, watching television. She has been told to keep out of your room so that she doesn't catch it, too. As she walks by the door, stare goggle-eyed at the TV:

"Oh my goodness! That's incredible! I've never seen anything like it in my life! I can't believe it! Wait till I tell the kids at school." Do not remove eyes from set, staring in amazement. "I wouldn't miss this for anything! I really don't believe it." Look at your sister. "What?" Move over on the bed. "Of course there's room for you."

Delia Ephron
How to Eat like a Child

MARAOLO
MARAOLO
MARAOLO
MARAOLO

Stories about My Sister

More revolutinary even than her theories about health was Aunt Helen's attitude toward our sisterhood. She was an only child, so she didn't really understand about sisters, but wasn't it crazy, she asked her friend, that her husband's family had raised two girls born ten months apart, and who were different in personality and temperment as if they were twins? . . . . I didn't like to think that Marie and I were different. There was no denying Marie was a reader and student who preferred sedentary activities, whereas I, who never cracked a book, was a tomboy.

And it was true that despite twin outfits we didn't really look alike. Also I could understand Marie's wish to separate herself from me when I showed insufficient daring, was a crybaby, or a copycat. (Recently, she'd found it pesky that when we went to buy ice cream cones after the movie, I wouldn't make up my mind what flavor I wanted until I heard her choice, and with maddening predictability said, "I'll have the same, please.")

As I listened to Aunt Helen talking to her friend, I couldn't see what was so wrong with people treating Marie and me as if we were alike.

Eileen Simpson
Orphans

Amy was a looker; I privately thought she must be the most beautiful child on earth. She inherited our father's thick, wavy hair. Her eyes were big, and so were her lashes; her nose was delicate and fluted, her skin translucent. Her mouth curved quaintly; her lips fitted appealingly, as a cutter's bow dents and curls the water under way. Plus she was quiet. And little, and tidy, and calm, and more or less obedient. She had an endearing way—it attracted even me—of standing with her legs tight together, and peering up and around with wild, stifled hilarity and parodied curiosity, as if to see if—by chance—anybody has noticed small her and found her amusing.

At the top of Richland Lane lived Amy's friend Tibby, a prematurely sophisticated blond tot, best remembered for having drawled conversationally to Mother, when she, Tibby, was only six and still missing her front teeth, "I love your hair, Mrs. Doak." When Tibby and Amy were eight, Amy brought home yet another straight-A report card. Shortly afterward, Mother overheard Tibby say exasperated to Amy, "How can you be so smart in school and so dumb after school?" In fact, as the years passed, after school became Amy's bailiwick, and she was plenty smart at it.

When Amy wasn't playing with Tibby, she played with her dolls. They were a hostile crew. Lying rigidly in their sick beds, they shot at each other a series of haughty expletives. She had picked these up from Katy Keene comic books; Katy Keene was a society girl with a great many clothes. Amy pronounced every consonant of these expletives: Humph, pshaw.

"I'll show you, you vixen!" cried a flat-out and staring piece of buxom plastic from its Naturlizer shoe box.

"Humph!"

"Pshaw!"

"Humph!"

"Pshaw!"

We all suffered a bit for want of more of these words.

Annie Dillard
An American Childhood

COLORS

You were yellow.
I was red, including pink and some
lavenders. If the lavenders
got too bluish, they were Tita's, our
blue sister, who could also have
green if she wanted. Our baby sister
wasn't even born yet, and
then she was mostly in white for a few
years until she started learning
her colors and wanted all of them for
herself. We were ingrained in
our colors; to this day, almost thirty
years later, I see a sunset,
and I think, yours.

Julia Alvarez
Yellow

*My sister Lettie was a
very pretty little girl with golden hair
and blue-grey eyes, an exquisite complexion,
a sweet and serious voice and a gentle
air which captivated adults . . .
I remember going to some sort of display at
the school my two elder sisters attended
and watching Lettie in a painful ecstacy as she
danced a solo, so lovely, so cool,
so innocent, twirling about as weightless as a
snowflake, her eyes set in the distance
and her lips slightly parted.*

Rebecca West
Family Memories

A sister
is both
your
mirror—
and
your
opposite.

◆

Elizabeth Fishel

Doren's Child

When Doren was three years old she informed our parents she had to have a baby sister. A year later I was born. Doren often reminded me I had her to thank for this. Was I supposed to feel grateful, needed, loved? I never quite knew, but I know I believed it was my sister's idea that I come into being. I came into the world, then, Doren's child.

Cathy Arden
My Sister's Picture

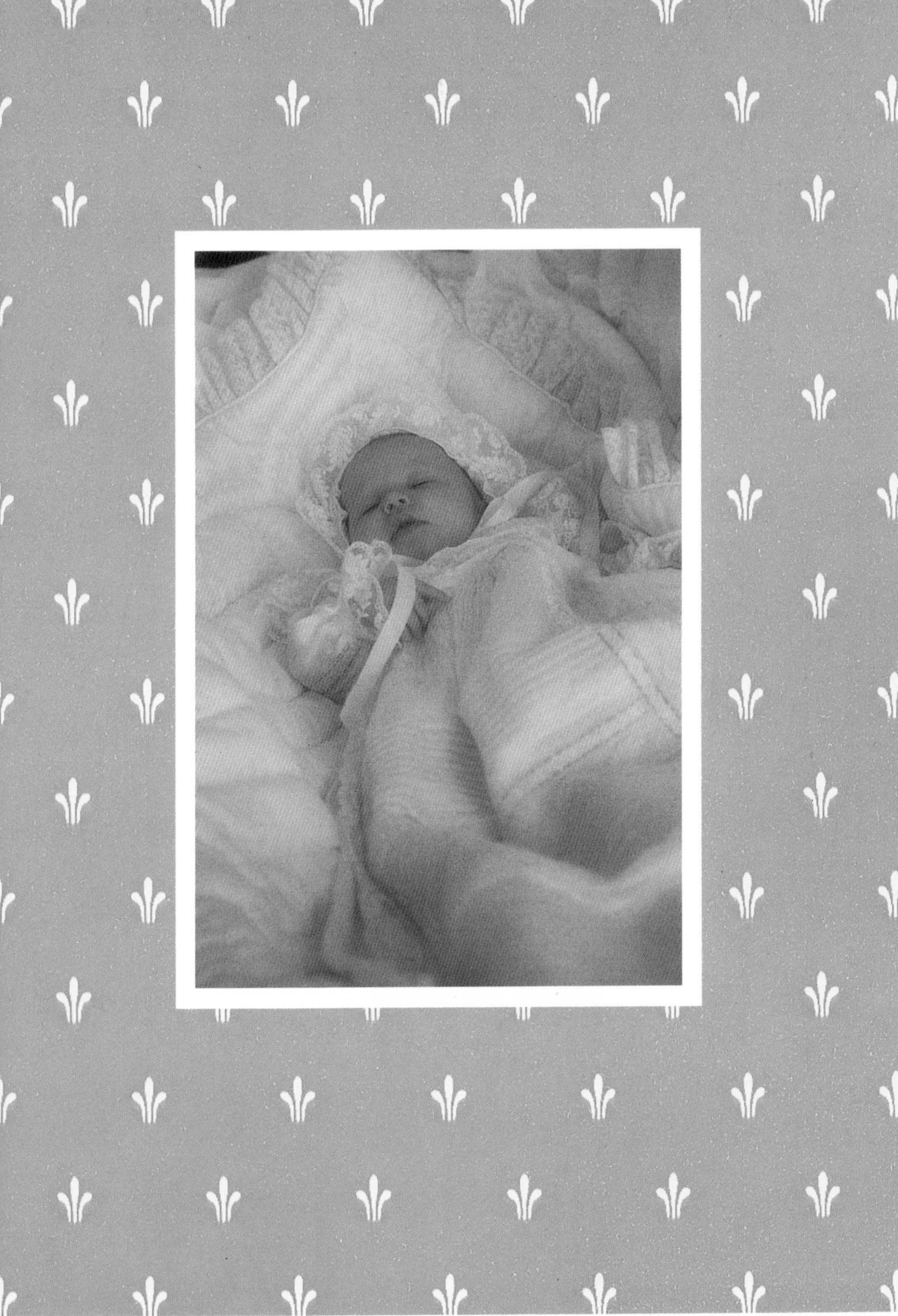

There is great abundance
of safe, healthful, and delightful
recreations, which all parents may
secure for their children . . . .
One of the most useful
and important, is the cultivation of
flowers and fruits. This,
especially for the daughters of a
family, is greatly promotive of health
and amusement . . . .

Catharine Beecher and Harriet Beecher Stowe
Gardening and the Education of Women

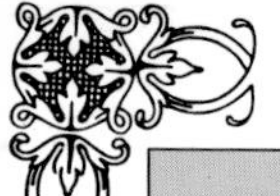

There is no time like the old time, when you and I were young!

Oliver Wendell Holmes

I hold this task to be
the highest task for a bond
between two people;
that each protects the solitude
of the other.

Rainer Maria Rilke

Where we love is home,
Home that our feet may leave,
but not our hearts.

Oliver Wendell Holmes
Homesick in Heaven

The House Where We Grew Up

Here is home.
An old thread,
long tangled,
comes straight again.

Marjorie Rawlings
Cross Creek

Victoria

According to popular myth, sisters exist on the same side of the closed door, sharing teddy bears and secrets in the privacy of a common bedroom.

Marianne Paul
Yin and Yang

W hat are the wild waves saying,
Sister, the whole day long?

Joseph Edwards Carpenter
What Are the Wild Waves Saying?

I had a mother of monumental will and dainty ways and two sisters, one a tomboy, the other a throwback in appearance to a bit of Indian ancestor. ... Our world was sleep and play and school, and our mother reading to us each night. From 7:00 to 8:00 P.M. in our house Robinson Crusoe worked on his leather umbrella. Sir Walter Scott's novels moved at their regal pace. Our mother read *Huckleberry Finn, The Illiad* and *The Odyssey, El Cid* (we knew each knight who sat at King Arthur's round table as well as we did our first cousins), and for my sisters she read *Little Women*. In time I became a full-blown romantic, never again to see things as they are. Or at least never again to see things as non-romantic people see them.

Clyde Rice
Leaving the Fold:
A Boyhood in Oregon

Books We Shared

Alice was getting very tired of sitting by her sister on the bank, and of having nothing to do: once or twice she peeped into the book her sister was reading, but it had no pictures or conversations in it, "and what is the use of a book," thought Alice, "without pictures or conversations?"

Lewis Carroll
Alice in Wonderland

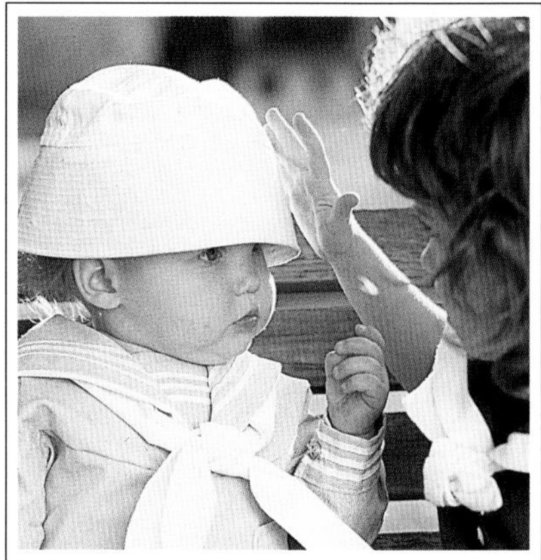

Childhood is from birth to a certain age and at a certain age
The child is grown, and puts away childish things.
Childhood is a kingdom where nobody dies.
Nobody that matters, that is.

Edna St. Vincent Millay

Between the dark and the daylight,

When the night is beginning to lower,

Comes a pause in the day's occupations,

That is known as the Children's Hour.

Henry Wadsworth Longfellow
The Children's Hour

Being Reverdy's Sister

You mustn't think she was like me. She wasn't in the least. Not inside or out. She had dark hair like a cloud. Yes, really. It wasn't curly, but it didn't hang straight. It billowed out. And her face—oh, you mustn't think it was anything like mine. She had hazel eyes and a pointed chin. And you've seen lots of people, haven't you, with very live animated faces and dead eyes? It was just the other way with Reverdy. Her face was always quiet, but her eyes were so alive they glowed. Oh, she was the most beautiful, most alive, and most most loved girl in the world, and she was my sister . . . .

I used to be awfully proud of her being my sister. I don't know what I would have done without her. I was a terribly plain little frump—I wore glasses and had freckles. If I hadn't been Reverdy's sister, I'd have had to sit and play jacks by myself, until Joe came along. But boys would try to get Reverdy's attention by doing things for me. They'd say to her, "Does your sister want to ride on my handlebars?" And Reverdy would say, all glowing, happier than if she'd been asked, "Do you, Sister?" Of course, I did, and when the boy came back, she'd ride with him just to thank him.

Jessamyn West
Reverdy

Give what you have. To someone, it may be better than you dare think

Henry Wadsworth Longfellow
Kavanagh

There is always one moment in childhood when the door opens and lets the future in.

Graham Greene
The Power and the Glory

My Sister's Gifts to Me

A RED COAT AND A BLUE

My sister was tall and lithe, with hair the shade of beautifully rubbed wood—chestnut I think my grandmother called it. Her eyes were a blue-green, and her skin English-fair with a dusting of freckles. I, on the other hand, was destined to be shorter, with darker hair and eyes the same deep brown that my son's are now. Armed with these genes, my grandmother insisted that my sister have a blue coat and I, a red.

For some reason this spring ritual is very prominent in my memory, even though we made a similar excursion in the fall and those heavier coats were also blue and red—just a deeper shade.

There was one advantage to my grandmother's system. Despite being the younger sister, I was never heir to my sister's coat from the year before, for her color was clearly not right for me. According to my grandmother, these garments, which we grew out of at an alarming rate, must have gone to cousins or friends who were selected because they had the appropriate eye and hair colors.

Over the years, my sister became "allergic" to blue and, to this day, refuses to wear it—especially outerwear. I must confess I think her reaction a bit excessive, particularly since I've always felt our grandmother had a way of knowing what was best in most things.

My own little tribute to her taste and determination is to always have at least one red coat in my wardrobe. I do not buy one each season or even each year, but ever in my closet is that bright note to remind me of the loving, caring woman who so dutifully went about the business of raising young ones with such assurance.

Jenny Walton

We had horses, too, one at a time and one that will remain forever in memory. A handsome beast, trained both for buggy and saddle, he was gentle but spooky. The slightest thing made him shy. Early in our experience with him my sister and I had been reading *Black Beauty*, with its emphasis on cruelty to animals. One of the cruelties was blinkers on bridles. Why, the poor horse couldn't see to the side much less behind him. At our urging and against his judgement, Father cut off the blinkers. Then a day or two afterward, we planned to take a drive, all of us, Father, Mother, and three children. Father hitched up. We got in the buggy. Father tapped Old Fox's rump with the reins and said "Get up." Old Fox took a step or two and then saw that something was following him, something right on his heels. With an explosion of wind that could be heard for miles, Old Fox leaped into a run. Around the lot we tore, Mother hanging on to little Chick, Father sawing at the reins, sister and I grabbing for handholds. On the second turn around the lot, Fox tangled a shaft in the fence and came to a stop, trembling violently. We didn't go for that planned drive. Somehow *Black Beauty* disappeared from the house.

A. B. Guthrie Jr.
A Small Town in Montana

'Anne, sister Anne,
do you see nothing coming?'
And her sister Anne replied,
'I see nothing but the sun making a dust,
and the grass looking green.'

Charles Perrault
Histoires et Contes du Temps Passé

The last time I visited my parents, I found a photograph from the 1950's of my two older sisters and me, in which we look very sisterly. We are dressed in identical polka-dotted pajamas with nightcaps to match, sitting lined up according to size on the living room floor. We look pretty silly, but the picture made me feel nostalgic anyway.

I remember that my middle sister was with me the day I purchased my first grown-up book. I was eleven and overwhelmed by the choices the bookstore offered me, until my sister helped me pick *Jane Eyre*. That same year, my oldest sister took me to Washington, D.C., the most sophisticated traveling I'd done up until then. I am still an avid buyer of books, and a traveler, who, like my sister, maps out most of the details before leaving home.

Paula Martinac
The One You Call Sister

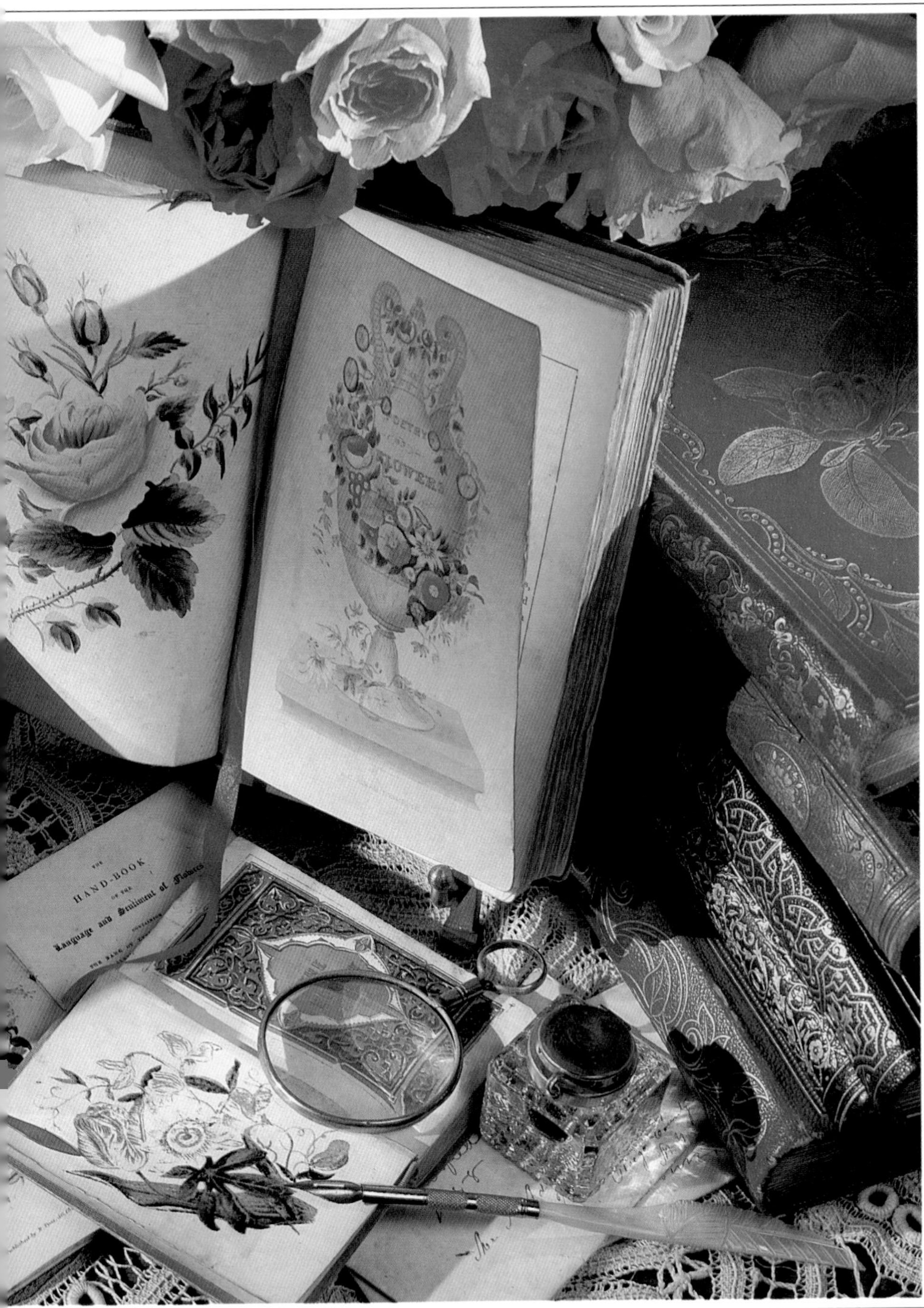
HAND-BOOK
Language and Sentiment of Flowers

Memories of School Days

The second child was my sister, Corinne, more than a year younger than I. Until well into our school years, I always thought of her as being fragile (which she never was), with her curls and neat silk bows and rustling starched dresses. Until we were old enough to go to school, one of our grandmothers, a former schoolteacher, lived with us. She taught us both to read before we entered school. While we were growing up, Corinne and I went through the usual sibling rivalries, each believing the other to be favored. After we went into the world on our own in different directions, we became supportive friends.

Dee Brown
It Was a Magical Time

Blest pair of Sirens, pledges of Heaven's joy,
Sphere-born harmonious sisters, Voice and Verse.

John Milton
At a Solemn Music

About this time I seemed very suddenly unwieldy and given to helpless giggles. No one told me this awkwardness was adolescence and would go away. Edie just as suddenly was grown-up. I have a snapshot of us aged fifteen and thirteen. She looks eighteen. I look ten; Edie in black satin slippers, flaring black dress, a hat with tiny ostrich plumes, I in socks, cotton dress with pleated skirt buttoned on, feet apart, Dutchbob, half a generation and a continent away. Not when, but would I ever get there? "Edith, what is a good complexion? Pink cheeks or white skin?" Apparently it was neither. "Edie, what do they mean when they say a good figure? Does that mean tall or is it thin?" She was not condescending, but surely in despair. No one ever told her—she just knew.

Irene Mayer Selznick
A Private View

MY SISTER'S BEAUTY

It was in Europe I think that I first recognized the quality of Ernesta's beauty. At home people took this for granted; certainly it made no marked impression on my brothers; I never heard them speak of it. But abroad we were among strangers, and moreover we were always together. "Is that beautiful girl your *sister*?" I would be asked . . . .

Women as well as men were forever offering handsome presents to Ernesta; it was a condition that lasted all her life. When we were young I considered her refusals quite crazy, and asked if she thought it would be "improper" to take these gifts. She said yes it would be improper, but the real reason was it wouldn't be *fair*. This silenced me. Anybody raised with four older brothers early learns what is fair and what is not. One's place in the pecking order depends on it, perhaps one's daily existence . . . .

By today's notions I should have been consumed with envy for my beautiful sister, expressed in silent rivalry, asthma, or loud recriminations and the striving for revenge. Rivalry however was out of the question; one might as well have tried to rival the moon. Occasionally the diary broke out: "Oh, if only I was pretty! I would give *anything* to be pretty." And again (at eleven), I wonder if I will be as gay and popular as Ernesta when I grow up. I don't believe I would like anything better. I know I won't, because I have no rich friends, like she has. Besides, I am

so shy that nobody would want to talk to me. I hope I will improve as I get older . . . ." It has taken me a half a century to realize it, but I think Mother possessed an inspired eye for the essence, the nature, of each of her six children and that she fostered what she saw. Mamma did not urge. Rather, it was as if she opened a door and said, Now child, walk through if you wish. Your world is there before you . . . . I could have been destroyed by my sister's beauty; there is no doubt Mamma recognized the danger. She kept us in separate worlds, so that from the first our friends and our ambitions were marked off and did not cross.

Catherine Drinker Bowen
Family Portrait

And so do his sisters,
and his cousins, and his aunts!
His sisters and his cousins,
Whom he reckons up by dozens,
And his aunts!

W.S. Gilbert
The Pirates of Penzance

My father's sister, Aunt Mary, had been a magnificent pianist, my mother said. Music ran in the family. She and my father liked concerts, and they had a small but prized collection of symphony records. On the piano was a thick volume of Gilbert and Sullivan songs, which my father especially liked. Gathering all these clues, I made an effort to include music in my own life. When, at twenty, I sat alone in a cheap seat at the Sadler's Wells Theatre in London and entered eagerly into the D'Oyly Carte's production of *The Mikado*, I kept a paperback copy of the lyrics in my lap. I didn't want to miss a word.

Susan Allen Toth
Missing: A Man with a Briefcase

*Caitlin nudged Sophie.
Mum was pouring a cup of tea. The
man next to her had a grayish-white spot
on the back of his dark head,
and Mum's eyes were lit with brightness.
When her sister Grace visited,
sitting on the porch in her smart wool
dresses and silk kerchiefs and
black sunglasses, telling New York stories,
Mum would get that look, giggling now
and then in an odd, excited way.*

Susan Minot
Monkeys

Cathy was easy to live with. At first she acted as if a mother was going to turn up to take care of her, but she soon got the hang of helping to clean up, and she got very involved with my cookbooks. She'd never cooked at home; my kitchen became her lab. She baked cookies for her classes and made dinner for us every night, sometimes for her brother and his wife as well. They came over often; she adored Larry and admired Joyce. He lapped up Cathy's cooking and loving attention; Joyce had to keep reminding him to watch his weight, for the sake of his heart, which is delicate. There was something warm and comfortable about the three of them together, tumbling over each other's sore points like kittens, landing harmlessly on their feet.

Linda Ostreicher
My Sister, My Eye

Recollections of My Sister

I had a sister much older than myself, from whose modesty and goodness, which were great, I learned nothing.

Saint Teresa

Mrs. Ludlow was the eldest of the three sisters, and was usually thought to be the most sensible; the classification being in general that Lilian was the practical one, Edith the beauty, and Isabel the 'intellectual' superior. Mrs. Keyes, the second of the group, was the wife of an officer of the United States Engineers . . . . Lilian had married a New York lawyer, a young man with a loud voice and an enthusiam for his profession; the match was not brilliant, any more than Edith's, but Lilian had occasionally been spoken of as a young woman who might be thankful to marry at all—she was so much plainer than her sisters. She was, however, very happy, and now, as the mother of two peremptory little boys and the mistress of a wedge of brown stone violently driven into Fifty-third Street, seemed to exult in her condition as in a bold escape. She was short and solid, and her claim to figure was questioned, but she was conceded presence, though not majesty; she had moreover, as people said, improved since her marriage, and the two things in life of which she was most distinctly conscious were her hus-

band's force in argument and her sister Isabel's originality. 'I've never kept up with Isabel—it would have taken *all* my time,' she had often remarked; in spite of which, however, she held her rather wistfully in sight; watching her as a motherly spaniel might watch a free greyhound. 'I want to see her safely married—that's what I want to see,' she frequently noted to her husband.

'Well, I must say I should have no particular desire to marry her,' Edmund Ludlow was accustomed to answer in an extremely audible tone.

'I know you say that for argument; you always take the opposite ground. I don't see what you've against her except that she's so original.'

'Well I don't like originals; I like translations,' Mr. Ludlow had more than once replied. 'Isabel's written in a foreign tongue. I can't make her out. She ought to marry an Armenian or a Portuguese.'

'That's just what I'm afraid she'll do!' cried Lilian, who thought Isabel capable of anything.

Henry James
Portrait of a Lady

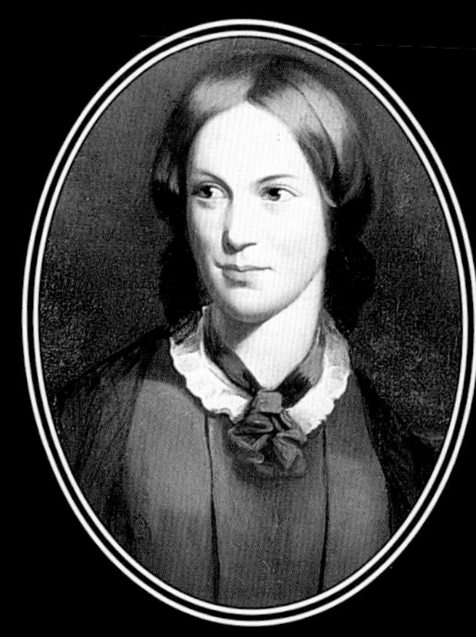

My sister Emily loved the moors. Flowers brighter than the rose bloomed in the blackest of the heath for her; out of a sullen hollow in a livid hill-side, her mind could make an Eden. She found in the bleak solitude many and dear delights; and not the least and best-loved was — liberty. Liberty was the breath of Emily's nostrils.

Charlotte Brontë

HER FAIR SISTER

Alice is tall and upright as a pine,
White as blanched almonds, or the falling snow,
Sweet as the damask roses when they blow
And doubtless fruitful as the swelling vine.
Ripe to be cut, and ready to be pressed,
Her full cheeked beauties very well appear,
And a year's fruit she loses every year,
Wanting a man to improve her to the best.

Full fain she would be husbanded, and yet,
Alas! she cannot a fit labourer get
To cultivate her to her won content:
Fain would she be (God wot) about her task,
And yet (forsooth) she is too proud to ask,
And (which is worse) too modest to consent.

Margaret of humbler stature by the head
Is (as it oft falls out with yellow hair)
Than her fair sister, yet so much more fair,
As her pure white is better mixed with red.
This, hotter than the other ten to one,
Longs to be put into her mother's trade,
And loud proclaims she lives too long a maid,
Wishing for one to untie her virgin zone.

She finds virginity a kind of ware,
That's very very troublesome to bear,
And being gone, she thinks will ne'er be missed:
And yet withal, the girl has so much grace,
To call for help I know she wants the face,
Though asked, I know not how she would resist.

Charles Cotton
Two Rural Sisters

Every large family had its designated "beauty," and in the Darden household that distinction went to Lizzie. Of all the girls, she was the most impetuous, flirtatious and popular with the boys. She was reputed to be one of the best dancers in the county, and Mama Darden saw to it that she was certainly one of the best dressed. Papa Darden and sons were very protective of Lizzie and discouraged gentlemen callers so that she would finish her education.

Lizzie's distinguishing talent was her dramatic recitation of poetry from memory. Her theatrical gestures and well-timed pauses kept her in demand with church groups and women's clubs in Wilson and neighboring towns who invited her to perform at their teas, testimonials, and concerts. However, Lizzie never contemplated the stage as a career; when it came time to pick an occupation, she chose nursing.

Norma Jean and Carole Darden
Spoonbread and Strawberry Wine

To her own heart,
which was shaped exactly
like a Valentine,
there came a winglike
palpitation, a delicate exigency,
and all the fragrance
of all the flowery
springtime love affairs
that ever were seemed
waiting for them...

Jean Stafford
Children Are Bored on Sunday

Holiday Traditions

Salem, Jany, 15, 1767

Dear Sister,

Your kind letter I reciev'd today and am greatly rejoiced to (hear) you are all so well. I was very uneasy at not hearing from you, indeed my dear Sister the Winter never seem'd so tedious to me in the World. I daily count the days between this and the time I may probably see you. I could never feel so comfortable as I at present do, if I thought I should spend another Winter here. Indeed my Sister I cannot bear the thought of staying here so far from all my Friends if Mr. Cranch can do as well nigher. I would give a great deal only to know I was within Ten Miles of you if I could not see you. Our children will never seem so natural to each other as if they liv'd where they could see one another oftener . . . .

Letter from *Mary Smith Cranch*
to her sister, Abigail Adams

Merry Xmas!

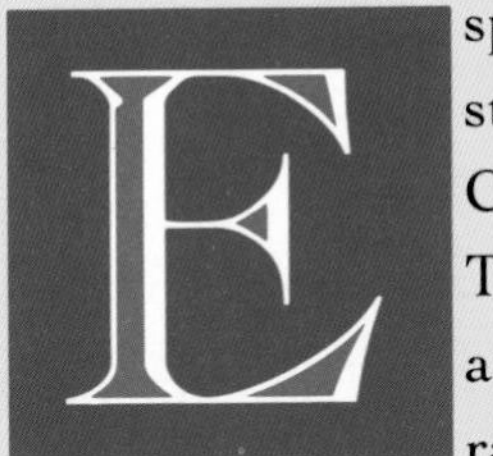

Esprit de corps has always run strong in our family but at Christmas it tends to run amok. Take the Christmas, probably around 1960, when we kids ranged in age from about five to mid-teens. In an excess of Christmas fellow feeling, Kathy made matching red and green plaid wool jumpers for Mom and the four of us sisters and matching vests for Dad and our brother, Gary. We wore our plaids in public, all seven of us, and formed an awesome sea of red and green. The plaid vests and jumpers were just one more family Christmas inspiration that made us feel part of an enchanted circle. The jumpers are long gone, but all the rest of our Christmas traditions are intact. They remind us that things don't have to change. Christmas carols sound the same as they did when we were little. Mom has made fruitcake, and we're all home again for the holidays, just like always. It's Christmas, and you can count on it.

Holly J. Burkhalter
A Midwestern Sisters' Christmas Book

Margaret, the eldest of the four, was sixteen, and very pretty, being plump and fair, with large eyes, plenty of soft, brown hair, a sweet mouth, and white hands, of which she was rather vain. Fifteen-year-old Jo was very tall, thin and brown, and reminded one of a colt; for she never seemed to know what to do with her long limbs, which were very much in her way. She had a decided mouth, a comical nose, and sharp, grey eyes, which appeared to see everything, and were by turns fierce, funny or thoughtful. Her long, thick hair was her one beauty; but it was usually bundled into a net, to be out of her way. Round shoulders had Jo, big hands and feet, a fly-away look to her clothes, and the uncomfortable appearance of a girl who was rapidly shooting up into a young woman and didn't like it. Elizabeth—or Beth, as everyone called her—was a rosy, smooth-haired, bright-eyed girl of thirteen, with a shy manner, a timid voice, and a peaceful expression, which was seldom disturbed. Her father called her "Little Tranquility," and the name suited her excellently; for she seemed to live in a happy world of her own, only venturing out to meet the few she trusted and loved. Amy, though the youngest, was a most important person,—in her own opinion at least. A regular snow-maiden, with blue eyes, and yellow hair, curling on her shoulders, pale and slender, and always carrying herself like a young lady, unmindful of her manners.

Louisa May Alcott
Little Women

The year I got married was the last year that our family assembled for a decent picture. There we are, lined up on the brick steps of the last large house my parents owned, a Carmel frame house with bougainvillaea, several blocks from the Pacific Ocean, where I forced my prospective husband to repropose to me—so we would have a sunset and ocean setting for the memory album.

My father is a bit heavier but still electrically handsome with curly eyebrows, a crooked front tooth and an expensive silk scarf in his breast pocket—probably plucked off the top of a pile of silk scarves from the shop he currently owned in Carmel. Next to him is Mother, wearing her

"good" dress, a tweed hand-me-down from a sister-in-law in Chicago, with a matching sweater with tweed buttons. She is smiling.

Then the rest of us—I am wearing a kilt skirt and sweater and looking hearty, sitting next to my almost husband, wearing tie and sport coat, looking young. I am holding Tony, only three at that time, on my lap. Tony was a blond, chisled child, with a curling half-smile, the Infant of Prague in short navy-blue pants, sweater and Peter Pan collar. Wendy and Cindy, oafishly preadolescent, are all legs and inexperience, not yet beautiful but laughing. They are in jumpers. My brother John, handsome in a Kennedy-esque way, in pressed flannels, oiled loafers, shirt and tie (the East Coast later sacrificed for the Michelangelo-in-leather look) beside his wife (also sacrificed seven years later), a slim, high-cheekboned blonde with cornsilk hair and blue eyes.

The clothes seem more important than the people in them. I am struck by how definite we all look, just as several years after, when I lined this photograph up with another later one, I was shocked to see how far and fast we had declined in style. Blue jeans, flyaway hair, everyone seated on aluminum chairs, without organization or thrust. The light is bright and bad. An unprofessional shot. But in 1963 when I got engaged and married, the family was still doing things right.

Phyllis Theroux
California and Other States of Grace

Celestine and Hortense had been drawn closely together in affection since they had come to live under the same roof, and they formed virtually one household . . . . The two sisters-in-law stayed at home and looked after their children together, and this had created a bond between them. They had come to be so close to each other that they spoke their thoughts aloud. They presented a touching picture of two sisters in harmony, one happy, the other sad. The unhappy sister, beautiful, charged with overflowing vitality, lively, gay, and quick witted, in appearance belied her actual situation; while the sober Celestine, so gentle and calm, as equable as reason itself, habitually reflective and thoughtful, would have made an observer believe that she had some secret sorrow. Perhaps the contrast between them contributed to their warm friendship: each found in the other what she lacked in herself.

Honoré de Balzac
Cousin Bette

She had come to be a friend and companion such as few possessed-intelligent, well-informed, useful, gentle, knowing all the ways of the family, interested in all its concerns, and peculiarly interested in Emma, in every pleasure, every scheme of hers; one to whom Emma could speak every thought as it arose, and who had such an affection for her as could never find fault.

Jane Austen
Emma

TO MY SISTER

My sister! ('tis a wish of mine)
Now that our morning meal is done,
Make haste, your morning task resign;
Come forth and feel the sun.

One moment now may give us more
Than years of toiling reason;
Our minds shall drink at every pore
The spirit of the season.

Then come, my Sister! Come, I pray,
With speed put on your woodland dress;
And bring no book: for this one day
We'll give to idleness.

William Wordsworth
To My Sister

THE REVENGE OF AN OLDER SISTER

There was once (said Reginald) a woman who told the truth. Not all at once, of course, but the habit grew upon her gradually like lichen on an apparently healthy tree. She had no children—otherwise it might have been different. It began with little things, for no particular reason except that her life was a rather empty one, and it is so easy to slip into the habit of telling the truth in little matters. And then it became difficult to draw the line at more important things, until at last she took to telling the truth about her age; she said she was forty-two and five months—by that time, you see, she was veracious even to months. It may have been pleasing to the angels, but her elder sister was not gratified. On the Woman's birthday, instead of opera-tickets which she had hoped for, her sister gave her a view of Jerusalem from the Mount of Olives, which is not quite the same thing. The revenge of an elder sister may be long in coming, but like a South-Eastern express, it arrives in its own good time.

Saki

The Woman Who Told the Truth

PARENTS
BE LIKE OLIVE PLANTS ROUND ABOUT THY
BIRTHS
MARRIAGES
HATH JOINED TOGETHER
LET NO MAN PUT ASUNDER
DEATHS
Sacred to the Memory of the Departed

And lovelier things have mercy shown
To every failing but their own;
And every woe a tear can claim,
Except an erring sister's shame.

Lord Byron
The Giaour

Comparison is a death knell
to sibling harmony.

Elizabeth Fishel

Never praise a sister to a sister, in the hope of your compliment ever reaching the proper ear.

Rudyard Kipling
Plain Tales from the Hills

Not being kissed at sixteen was harder for me to endure than it otherwise would have been because Ramona, my twelve-year-old sister, had been. She had had boy friends since she was ten. She had big boys of fifteen hanging around her from whom I would have been proud to have a glance. They treated me like Ramona's old-maid aunt. My brother Neddie was only sixteen months younger than I. When we were together where people didn't know us, I sidled up to him in a way I hoped onlookers would think romantic. To this day, Neddie still sits across the room from me when we visit. That year of sidling has made him permanently wary.

Jessamyn West
The Second (or Perhaps Third) Time Around

Sisterhood is powerful.

Robin Morgan

Thoughts on Being a Sister

Oh, I've erred and I have stumbled," Macon's sister sang in the kitchen, "I've been sinful and unwise . . ."

She had a tremulous soprano that sounded like an old lady's, although she was younger than Macon. You could imagine such a voice in church, some country kind of church where the women still wore flat straw hats . . . for there was something vague about her that caused her brothers to act put-upon and needy whenever she chanced to focus on them. She was pretty in a sober, prim way, with beige hair folded unobtrusively at the back of her neck where it wouldn't be a bother. Her figure was a very young girl's, but her clothes were spinsterly and concealing . . . .

There had always been some family member requiring Rose's care. Their grandmother had been bedridden for years before she died, and then their grandfather got so senile, and first Charles and later Porter had failed in their marriages and come back home. So she had enough right here to fill her time. Or she made it enough; for surely it couldn't be necessary to polish every piece of silver every week. Shut in the house with

her all day, Macon noticed how painstakingly she planned the menus; how often she reorganized the utensil drawer; how she ironed even her brother's socks, first separating them from the clever plastic grips she used to keep them mated in the washing machine. For Macon's lunch, she cooked a real meal and served it on regular place mats. She set out cut-glass dishes of pickles and olives that had to be returned to their bottles later on. She dolloped homemade mayonnaise into a tiny bowl.

Macon wondered if it ever occurred to her that she lived an odd sort of life—unemployed, unmarried, supported by her brothers. But what job would she be suited for? he asked himself. Although he could picture her, come to think of it, as the mainstay of some musty, antique law firm or accounting firm. Nominally a secretary, she would actually run the whole business, arranging everything just so on her employer's desk every morning and allowing no one below her or above her to overlook a single detail. Macon could use a secretary like her. Recalling the gum-chewing redhead in Julian's disastrous office, he sighed and wished the world had more Roses.

Anne Tyler
The Accidental Tourist

MY MOTHER'S SISTERS

In the early part of my childhood, I did not know any of my relatives, because they lived in Nova Scotia, two thousand miles away. My parents had left Nova Scotia during the Depression because there were no jobs there; by the time I was born, the Second World War had begun, and nobody traveled great distances without official reasons and gas coupons. But although my two aunts were not present in the flesh, they were very much present in the spirit. The three sisters wrote one another every week, and my mother read these letters out loud, to my father but by extension to myself and my brother, after dinner. They were called "letters from home . . . ."

But it was not my invisible aunts in their present-day incarnation who made the most impression on me. It was my aunts in the past. There they were as children, in the impossible starched and frilled dresses and the floppy satin hair bows of the first decades of the century, or as shingle-haired teenagers, in black and white in the photograph album, wearing strange clothing—cloche hats, flapper coats up over the knee—standing beside antique motor cars, or posed in front of rocks or the sea in striped bathing suits that came halfway down their legs. Sometimes their arms would be around one another. They have been given captions, by my mother, in white pencil on the black album pages: "We Three," "Bathing Belles." Aunt J. was thin as a child, dark-eyed, intense. Aunt K., the middle sister, looked tailored and brisk, in a Dutch cut. My mother, with huge pre-Raphaelite eyes and wavy hair and models' cheekbones, was the beauty, an assessment she made light of . . . . But all three sisters had the same high-bridged noses; Roman noses, my mother said. I pored over these pictures, intrigued by the idea of the triplicate, identical noses. I did not have a sister myself, then,and the mystique of sisterhood was potent for me.

Margaret Atwood
Growing Up With My Mother's Sisters

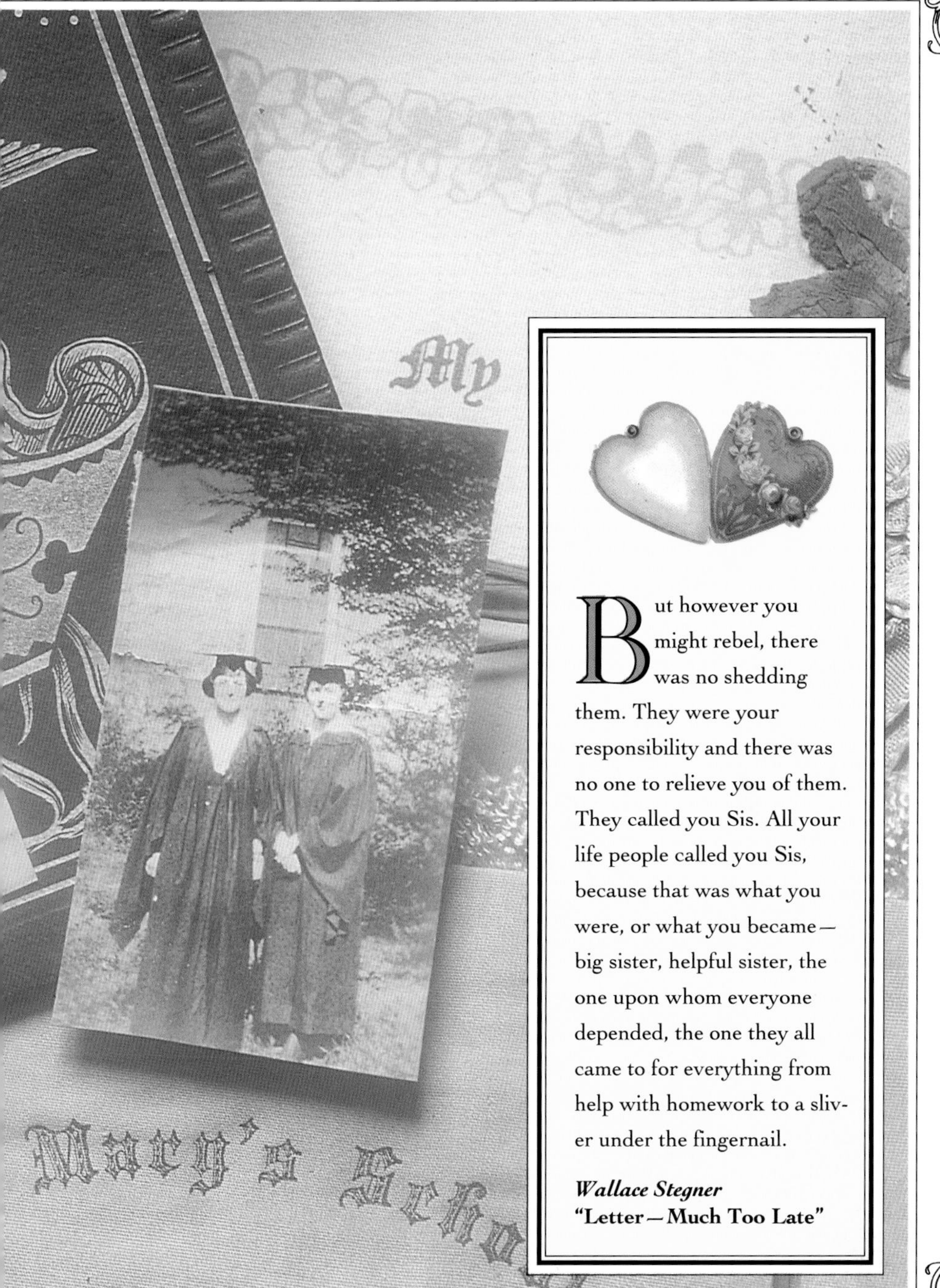

But however you might rebel, there was no shedding them. They were your responsibility and there was no one to relieve you of them. They called you Sis. All your life people called you Sis, because that was what you were, or what you became—big sister, helpful sister, the one upon whom everyone depended, the one they all came to for everything from help with homework to a sliver under the fingernail.

Wallace Stegner
"Letter—Much Too Late"

Their neighbors cannot recall a time when Glady Joe and Hy were not "old." It seemed that the two sisters had always been languishing somewhere in their senior years, as if they had somehow executed the leap from girlhood to middle age to senior citizen, lacking any sort of transitional areas in between. And it seemed that one was seldom seen without the other. Except for that brief time following the death of Hy's husband, James Dodd, but that was a short period and soon all appeared to be back as it was. Even married, the two sisters never lived apart. These days they share the house where the quilting circle meets, where Glady Joe had lived with her husband, Arthur Cleary, also deceased. When Arthur was alive, before Hy moved in, the house held their twins, Francie and Kayo, as well as Anna Neale, their housekeeper, and her daughter, Marianna. Anna said, "This is a strange house; haunted, I think it could be said. But it is an odd haunting, not as if something extra were here as much as something missing; not a void, only the powerful absence of a thing lost."

Whitney Otto
How to Make an American Quilt

The weird sisters, hand in hand,
Posters of the sea and land,
Thus do go about, about.

William Shakespeare
Macbeth

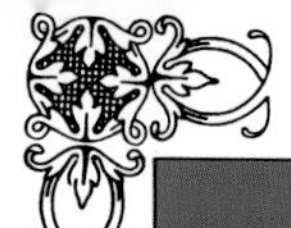

For my own part,
though: it would have been catastrophic
if I had forgotten my sister at once.
I had never told her so, but she
was the person I had always written for. She
was the secret of whatever artistic
unity I had ever achieved. She was the
secret of my technique. Any creation which
has any wholeness and harmoniousness,
I suspect, was made by an artist or inventor
with an audience of one in mind.
Yes, and she was nice enough, or Nature
was nice enough, to allow me to
feel her presence for a number of years after
she died—to let me go on writing
for her. But then she began to fade away,
perhaps because she had more important
business elsewhere.

Kurt Vonnegut
Slapstick

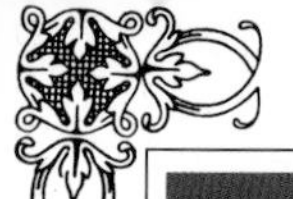

The Moon on the one hand, the Dawn on the other;

The Moon is my sister, the Dawn is my brother.

The Moon on my Left and the Dawn on my Right.

My Brother, good morning; my Sister good night.

Hilaire Belloc
The Early Morning

PERMISSIONS AND PHOTO CREDITS

6: Photograph courtesy of Lalah Lewellen.

8-9: Antique postcard courtesy of Nina Ovryn Design.

10: Inset photograph by Michael Skott. Background photograph by Toshi Otsuki.

11: Photograph by Luciana Pampalone.

12-13: Inset photograph by Wendi Schneider. Background photograph by Toshi Otsuki.

14: Photograph by Elyse Lewin.

15: Photograph by Bryan E. McCay.

16-17: Photograph by Monica Roberts.

18: Photograph by Toshi Otsuki.

19: Excerpt from *One Writer's Beginning* by Eudora Welty. Copyright © 1983, 1984 by Eudora Welty. Reprinted by permission of Harvard University Press.

20: Inset photograph by Tom Hooper. Background photograph by Luciana Pampalone.

22: Photograph by Monica Roberts. Excerpt from *Household Words* by Joan Silber. Copyright © 1976, 1980 by Joan Silber. Reprinted by permission of Viking Penguin, a division of Penguin Books USA, Inc.

23: Excerpt from *Life: A Warning by Stephanie Brush*. Copyright © 1987 by Stephanie Brush. Reprinted by permission of Linden Press, a division of Simon & Schuster, Inc.

24-25: Inset photograph by Sandra Eisner. Background photograph by Tina Mucci.

26: Photograph by Tina Mucci.

28: Photograph by Toshi Otsuki. Excerpt from *The Prince of Tides* by Pat Conroy. Copyright © 1986 by Pat Conroy. Reprinted by permission of Houghton Mifflin Co.

30-31: Photograph by Bryan E. McCay.

32-33: Photograph by Toshi Otsuki. Excerpt from *How to Eat Like A Child* by Delia Ephron. Copyright © 1988 by Delia Ephron. Reprinted by permision of Viking Penguin, a division of Penguin Books USA, Inc.

34: Photograph by Toshi Otsuki.

35: Excerpt from *Orphans: Real and Imaginery* by Eileen Simpson. Copyright © 1987 by Eileen Simpson. Reprinted by permission of Grove Press, Inc.

36: Photograph courtesy of Nina Ovryn Design. Excerpt from *An American Childhood* by Annie Dillard. Copyright © 1987 by Annie Dillard. Reprinted by permission of HarperCollins Publishers.

37: Photograph by Jeff McNamara.

38: Photograph by Tim Beddow.

39: Excerpt from "Yellow" by Julia Alvarez as reprinted in *The One You Call Sister,* edited by Paula Martinac, published by Cleis Press. Copyright © 1982 by Julia Alvarez. Reprinted by permission of the author.

40-41: Photographs by Toshi Otsuki. Excerpt from *Family Memories* by Rebecca West. Copyright © 1987 by Rebecca West. Reprinted by permission of Viking Penguin, a division of Penguin Books USA, Inc.

42-43: Photograph by Starr Ockenga.

45: Photograph by Stephen H. Moody.

46: Photograph by William P. Steele.

47: Photograph by Wendi Schneider.

48: Photograph by Pamela Barkentin.

49: Photograph by Bryan E. McCay.

51: Photograph by Toshi Otsuki.

52: Photograph by Ralph Bogertman.

53: Photograph of Ophelia the Bear from *Constant Friends* published by Viking Penguin, a division of Penguin Books USA, Inc.

54-55: Photograph by Elyse Lewin.

56: Photograph by William P. Steele.

57: Excerpt from "Leaving the Fold: A Boyhood in Oregon" by Clyde Rice as reprinted in *Growing Up Western,* edited by Clarus Baches. Copyright © 1986 by Alfred A. Knopf, Inc. Reprinted by permission of Random House, Inc.

58-59 Photograph by Lilo Raymond.

60: Photographs clockwise from top left by Elyse Lewin, Toshi Otsuki, Elyse Lewin, Nina Ovryn Design.

61: Photographs by Elyse Lewin. Bottom left photograph by Sue Daley.

62-63: Photograph by Elyse Lewin.

64-65: Top left artwork "Day Lilies" by David Griffin. Background photograph by Lilo Raymond. Excerpt from "Reverdy" b Jessamyn West from *The Collected Stories o Jessamyn West*. Copyright © 1986 by Har Maxwell McPherson. Reprinted by perm sion of Harcourt Brace Jovanovich, Inc.

68: Photograph by William P. Steele

70: Excerpt from "A Red Coat and Blue" by Jenny Walton as printed in *Vict* magazine. Reprinted by permission of the author.

72-73: Photograph by Sanders Nicolso courtesy of J. Barbour & Sons, Ltd. Exce from "A Small Town in Montana" by A.B Guthrie, Jr. as reprinted in *Growing Up Western* edited by Clarus Baches. Copyrig © 1986 by Alfred A. Knopf, Inc. Reprinte by permission of Random House, Inc.

74: Photograph by Bryan E. McCay

76-77: Photograph by Starr Ockenga. Excerpt from "Introduction" by Paula Martinac from *The One You Call Sister* edit by Paula Martinac, published by Cleis Press. Copyright © 1989 by Paula Martin Reprinted by permission of the author.

78: Photograph by Tina Mucci.

79: Excerpt from "It Was A Magical Time" by Dee Brown as from *Growing Up Western,* edited by Clarus Baches. Copyright © 1986 by Alfred A. Knopf, Inc. Reprinted by pemission of Random House, Inc.

80-81: Inset photograph by Tina Mucci.

82: Inset photograph by Toshi Otsuki Background photograph by Elyse Lewin. .

83: Excerpt from *A Private View* by Irene Mayer Selznick. Copyright © 1983 by Irene Mayer Selznick. Reprinted by permission of Alfred A. Knopf, Inc.

84-85: Photograph by Toshi Otsuki. Excerpt from *Family Portrait* by Catherine Drinker Bowen. Copyright © 1970 by Catherine Drinker Bowen. Reprinted by permission of Little, Brown and Co.

86: Photograph courtesy of Nina Ovryn Design.

87: Excerpt from "Missing: A Man with a Briefcase" by Susan Allen Toth from *Family Portraits: Remembrances of Twenty Celebrated Writers,* edited by Carolyn Anthony. Copyright © 1989 by Carolyn Anthony. Reprinted by permission of Doubleday, a division of the Bantam, Doubleday, Dell Publishing Group, Inc.

88: Photograph by Toshi Otsuki.

89: Excerpt from *Monkeys* by Susan Minot. Copyright © 1987 by Susan Minot.

90: Excerpt from "My Sister, My Eye" by Linda Ostreicher from *The One You Call Sister* edited by Paula Martinac, published by Cleis Press. Reprinted by permission of the author.

91: Photograph by Tina Mucci.

92-93: Photograph by Zeva Oelbaum.

94-95: Background photograph by Starr Ockenga.

96-97: Background photograph by William P. Steele.

98: Photograph by Toshi Otsuki.

100-101: Background photograph by Jim Heidrich. Inset photograph by Toshi Otsuki. Excerpt from *Spoonbread and Strawberry Wine* by Norma Jean and Carole Darden. Copyright © 1978 by Norma Jean and Carole Darden. Reprinted by permission of Doubleday, a division of Bantam, Doubleday, Dell Publishing Group, Inc.

102: Photograph by Bryan E. McCay.

104: Photograph courtesy of Nina Ovryn Design.

106: Photograph courtesy of Nina Ovryn Design.

107: Excerpt from *Four Midwestern Sisters' Christmas Book* by Holly J. Burkhalter. Copyright © 1991 by Holly J. Burkhalter. Reprinted by permission of Viking Penguin, a division of Penguin Books USA, Inc.

108: Photographs from a collage of vintage advertisements by Starr Ockenga.

112: Photograph by Steve Gross.

114-115: Photograph by Toshi Otsuki.

116: Photograph by Michael Boys.

119: Photograph by Starr Ockenga.

120-121: Photograph by Toshi Otsuki.

122: Photograph by Irene Chang.

124-125: Photograph by Starr Ockenga. Excerpt from *The Accidental Tourist* by Anne Tyler. Copyright © 1985 by Anne Tyler Modarressi. Reprinted by permission of Random House, Inc.

126: Excerpt from "Growing Up With My Mother's Sisters" by Margaret Atwood in *Family Portraits: Remembrances of Twenty Celebrated Writers,* edited by Carolyn Anthony. Copyright © 1989 by Carolyn Anthony. Reprinted by permission of Doubleday a division of the Bantam, Doubleday, Dell Publishing Group, Inc.

127: Photograph courtesy of Alice Evans.

128-129: Photograph by Toshi Otsuki. Excerpt from "Letter—Much Too Late" by Wallace Stegner in *Family Portraits: Remembrances of Twenty Celebrated Writers,* edited by Carolyn Anthony. Copyright © 1989 by Carolyn Anthony. Reprinted by permission of Doubleday a division of Bantam, Doubleday, Dell Publishing Group, Inc.

130: Inset photograph by Lilo Raymond. Background photograph by Toshi Otsuki.

131: Excerpt from *How to Make an American Quilt* by Whitney Otto. Copyright © 1991 by Whitney Otto. Reprinted by permission of Random House, Inc.

132-133: Photograph of nymphs at the Untermyer Fountain by Toshi Otsuki in Conservatory Garden, Central Park.

134: Photograph by Ross Chapple.

135: Excerpt from *Slapstick* by Kurt Vonnegut. Copyright © 1976 by Kurt Vonnegut. Reprinted by permission of Delacorte Press/Seymour Lawrence, a division of Bantam, Doubleday, Dell Publishing Group, Inc.

136-137: Photograph by Toshi Otsuki.

FIN

Victoria

NO FRIEND LIKE A SISTER